Dreams
Working Words of Wit and Wisdom

By Robert W. Pike

Art By Cindi Sonntag

Published by
Resources for Organizations, Inc.
7251 Flying Cloud Drive
Eden Prairie, MN 55344
(612) 829-1954

ISBN 1-56447-012-1

Foreword

by Robert W. Pike

This book has been a labor of love. It stems from the desire to help trainers and others who do presentations be more creative in their approach to visuals. Visuals, you see, should be visual. Yet 80% of the business slides produced in North America are not visual at all - they are simply pictures of words.

Each of the quotes illustrated here was carefully chosen - was it positive, uplifting, did it make a point - frequently with humor. Next - could it be represented in clear visual form? We could have stopped there, but we didn't. For many that I've used in my own presentations, I've included some thought-starters and comments that might stimulate your own thinking about possible uses.

This volume was designed to be flexible. You'll note that we've given you the limited right to use the visuals without worrying about infringing our copyright. Make a photocopy and use it to create a transparency. Blow it up, color it, and make a poster. Use it to add spice to your presentation - or inspiration to you classroom or office.

For a change of pace show a group a visual and have them make their own application. You might be amazed at the power in that one small suggestion. So, enjoy this book and use the working words of wit and wisdom to enrich yourself and those you come in contact with in your own journey through life.

Robert W. Pike

Acknowledgments

This book was made possible because of a group of people who together breathe life into Creative Training Techniques International. Audrey, who provides the supportive environment that helps others develop. Judy and Mary, who support their teams. Lisa and Julie, who see to it that materials are ordered and delivered. Brenda, who makes sure that the bookkeeping gets down in an organized manner. Sherran who makes sure people get registered for our training programs. Donna who works with hundreds of hotels each year to make sure we have the best space possible to train in. And Sandi, who continues to master the complexities of desktop publishing to improve all our materials.

Our trainers and consultants are the best and continue their commitment to grow. Lynn, Doug, Lori, Michele, Tim, and Rich are committed to delivering training that empowers participants. It shows in their presentations and evaluations. And finally Cindi, who has shown an exceptional ability to visualize and turn words into pictures - and not only pictures but pictures that touch the heart. To each of you I say thank you.

The Next Volume

Is now under development. Do you have a quote you'd like to see illustrated? Send it to me, along with a source and we'll consider it for the next volume.

Related Products

Would you like to use this as a color transparency, but don't have the equipment - or how about a poster? Contact us to obtain either posters or transparencies of any of these visuals.

Creative Training Techniques International, Inc.
7251 Flying Cloud Drive
Eden Prairie, MN 55344
(612) 829-1954 or (612) 829-0260 fax

Law 1. Adults Are Babies With Big Bodies.

Recall the kinds of learning activities we did as small children, In kindergarten, we colored, drew, played games, modeled with clay, fingerpainted, etc.--all hands-on activities. Children with very little experience learn through experience.

When we reached first, second, and third grade, we lined up in rows, and we were talked at. Rarely were we encouraged, or even permitted, to be involved in the learning process. The more experience we had, the less that experience was used. As adults, we bring a lot of experience to our training programs. We want to acknowledge, honor, and celegrate that experience. If, as children with very little experience, we could discover and learn, how much more as adults can we discover and learn.

Adults are babies with big bodies.

—Pike's First Law

Law 2. People Don't Argue With Their Own Data.

If I say something is true, you might say to yourself, "He's got to believe it; he's teaching it." But if you say it, for you it's true.

For example, through research we might identify 15 characteristics of an effective leader. But rather than presenting them, I might choose to have small groups discuss the most effective leaders they've ever known and identify the characteristics that made those leaders effective. Normally, the groups will come up with 80 percent of the characteristics. It's easy for the instructor to fill in the other 20 percent. And I find the group much more willing to accept my suggestions for that remaining 20 percent than if I try to present all of them.

That's why I also compile action-idea lists in my seminars. I ask participants to look for ideas, concepts, and techniques for which they see an immediate use back on their jobs. From time to time, I'll ask volunteers to share the ideas they've picked up. It reinforces the value of the training and demonstrates, again, that people don't argue with their own data. Whether it's a technical course, management course, or sales course, the concept works. People look for the things they can use back on the job.

People don't argue with their own data.

—Pike's Second Law

Law 3. Learning Is Directly Proportional To The Amount Of Fun You Have.

I'm not referring here to jokes or pointless games or entertainment. I'm referring to the joy of learning that can come from involvement and participation. From realizing that you can use your own energy to learn-and enjoy learning because you're gaining information, tools, techniques, etc., that can benefit you. These acquisitions are going to help you do your job faster, better, easier, and they're going to help you solve problems.

Few of us have the entertainment skills of Bob Hope, John Cleese, Bill Cosby, or Joan Rivers. Few of us are able to keep the riveted attention of an audience for hours. Fortunately, we don't have to. We can use the energy, involvement, and participation of our audience to put into their personal learning experiences the excitement they vicariously get from some of their entertainment activities.

Humor itself, the kind that produces genuine, heartfelt laughter, can enhance the learning that takes place. One only has to read Norman Cousins' **Anatomy of an Illness** to realize that humor can aid enormously in reducing stress and anxiety, allowing people to relax and be more open to the learning process. That kind of humor should make a point and not simply provide amusement. Used judiciously, it should enhance the learning process and enable participants to derive greater benefit.

Learning is directly proportional to the amount of fun you are having.

—Pike's Third Law

Law 4. Learning Hasn't Taken Place Until Behavior Has Changed.

In training, it's not what you know but what you do with what you know that counts. That's why skill practice is so important in our training sessions. If we want people to do things differently, we must provide them with many opportunities to be comfortable accepting new ideas in a nonthreatening environment. It's one thing to know something intellectually; it's quite another to have the emotional conviction that comes from personal experience.

C.S. Lewis, the English philosopher, said, "A man with an experience is never at the mercy of a man with an argument." Today, he probably would have said "person" but his point would be the same: Give people success experiences in using our information and techniques in whatever learning environment we have available so that we increase the likelihood of on-the-job application.

Learning has not taken place until behavior has changed.

—Pike's Fourth Law

9

Law 5. FuYu, Wu Yu, Wzu Tu Yu

Roughly translated this means: Momma's having it or Papa's having it ain't like baby having it. If I can do something, so what" That's like Momma's having it. If you, as one of my participants, can do something, so what" That's like Papa's having it. It's when you can pass what you've learned on to someone else that I, as a trainer, know I've really done my job.

This law may seem silly, but in my seminars and in this handbook I'm using that silliness to make a serious point: It doesn't matter what I can do or what I can teach you to do. Ultimately what matters is what I can teach you to teach others to do. This is one confirmation of your competence--when you can pass what you know on to someone else.

"Fu Yu, Wu Yu, Wzu Tu Yu."
Translation:
*"Mama's havin' it
and Papa's havin' it
ain't like Baby havin' it."*

—Pike's Fifth Law

I use not only the brain I have, but all I can borrow.

It's been said that the biggest room in the world is the room for improvement. We're all either growing or dying. Moving ahead or falling back. There's no standing still. For a few dollars (or free if you use the library!) you can have the best experts best thoughts on any subject.

I use not only
the brain I have
but all I can borrow.

—Woodrow Wilson

13

Why not go out on a limb? Isn't that where the fruit is?

With risk goes reward. Thomas Edison once said that 90%
of all failures would have succeeded if they'd kept on
trying. Stretch a little today. Reach a little further than
you have before. Look for a new way to reach the fruit.

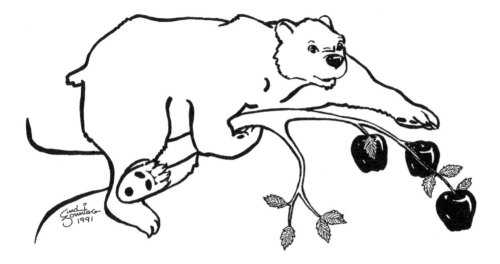

Why not go out on a limb?
Isn't that where the fruit is?

—Frank Scully

Some people are too tired to give you a smile. Give them one of yours. No one needs a smile so much as the one who has no more to give.

There's a proverb that says "A merry heart does good, like a medicine" and in Mary Poppins, we hear "A spoonful of sugar makes the medicine go down." When everything's gone wrong in a day there's nothing like a kind word and a smile to lift the heart. Not to solve the problem or wish it away, but just to say "I Care". Who can you share a smile with today?

Some people are too tired
to give you a smile.
Give them one of yours.
No one needs a smile so much as
the one who has no more to give.

—Anonymous

GENUINE SMILE
ONE SIZE FITS ALL!

Celebrate what you want to see more of.

Michael LeBonef says that the greatest management principle in the world is "what gets recognized gets done and what gets rewarded gets repeated." William James, the Harvard Psychologist said, "The greatet need of every human being is the need for appreciation." Who can you recognize and affirm today?

*Celebrate what
you want to
see more of.*

—Anonymous

Before you build a better mousetrap, it helps to know if there are any mice out there.

We've all heard the quote "Find a need and fill it." The roar of apathy may be loud and long if we don't look at what is needed and wanted. When we look at the problems people have, the pains they want to make go away and we find solutions to their problems and ways to eliminate their pain - then we won't have to worry about whether what we have is needed.

Before you build a better mousetrap, it helps to know if there are any mice out there.

—Mortimer B. Zucherman

No matter what accomplishments you make, someone helps you.

The President of General Motors said,"It's amazing what can be accomplished if you don't care who gets the credit." Are we as careful to give credit and to share it when we are in the limelight? Are we careful to remember the help we GIVE as well as the help we receive?

No matter what accomplishments you make, somebody helps you.

—Wilma Rudolph

Advice from a veteran trapeze performer: "Throw your heart over the bars and your body will follow."

The most powerful emotion in the world is love. Love can cause us to conquer fears, overcome pain, face conflict. Passion ignites enthusiasm and gives us focus. Where is your heart in your career? Where is your heart in your personal life?

Advice from a
veteran trapeze performer:
"Throw your heart
over the bars and
your body will follow."

I praise loudly, I blame softly.

The awesome power of the listening ear. No one is looking for a good talker. When did you have 15 minutes free and say to yourself "I wish I had someone to listen to"? No, we're looking for someone to listen to us. Listeners not only learn, they also lead and there is power in their voices when they speak.

I PRAISE LOUDLY.

I blame softly.

—Anonymous

Contentment: The smother of invention.

Contentment is the smother of improvements. Some people ask "Is everything OK?" Try asking instead, "What's one thing I could do better next time."

Contentment:
The smother
of invention.

—Ethel Mumford

It's easy to come up with new ideas; the hard part is letting go of what worked for you two years ago, but has become out of date.

Life is not static. Very few environments are static. Change occurs almost constantly. It's important to constantly analyze what's happening right now to make sure that our responses, approaches, processes, and products, are as appropriate today as they were two years ago.

*It's easy to come up with new ideas;
the hard part is letting go of what
worked for you two years ago, but
will soon be out-of-date.*

—Roger von Oech

Let your advance worrying become advance thinking & planning.

It's been said that worry is payment on a debt you may not owe. If there's a problem analyze it, seek solution, implement, correct and adjust. More problems are left unsolved by no action than by wrong action.

Let your advance worrying become advance thinking and planning.

—Winston Churchill

Great ideas need landing gear, as well as wings.

We need each other's differences. Some of us may be
great initiators, but we need completers too. Each of us
can supply what the other needs.

Great ideas need landing gear as well as wings.

—C.D. Jackson

We didn't all come over on the same ship, but we're all in the same boat.

The world grows smaller every day. In every country, state
or province, city and town there's diversity. We need each
others differences. Each of us has strengths to contribute.
Each of us can make up for another's lack. Together we
can solve problems that alone we can't. It starts by recog-
nizing that we're all in the same boat and a problem for
one becomes a problem for all.

We didn't all come over in the same ship, but we're all in the same boat.

—Bernard M. Baruch

Breakdowns can create breakthroughs. Things fall apart so things can fall together.

Napoleon Hill said "In every adversity lies the seed of an equivalent or greater benefit." Sometimes we get complacent. When things go well it's easy to coast. A breakdown may be just what we need to stimulate us, shake us up - and create the change we need.

Breakdowns can create breakthroughs. Things fall apart so things can fall together.

Anonymous

*Don't pray for dreams
equal to your powers.
Pray for powers equal
to your dreams.*

Money never starts an idea; it is the idea that starts the money.

It's easy to think that money will make an idea fly, but no amount of money will turn a bad idea into a good one. On the other hand good ideas can take off on wings of their own - money only speeds the flight. If money is the only thing stopping you - it may not be the only thing stopping you. Great ideas create their own energy and passion.

Money
never starts an idea;

it is the idea
that starts the money.

—W.J. Cameron

When one door closes, another opens; but we often look so long and so regretfully upon the closed door that we do not see the one which has opened to us.

This is the vacuum principle. To grow and go we need to create a vacuum. Do you want more clothes? Clean out a closet and get rid of what you don't need, want, or use. We need to let go of what we are grasping to take hold of something new.

When one door closes, another opens; but we often look so long and so regretfully upon the closed door that we do not see the one which has opened for us.

—Alexander Graham Bell

*Leadership is action,
not position.*

Donald H. McGannon

Imagination is more important than knowledge.

Robert F. Kennedy said "Some men look at things the way they are and ask why? I dream of things that are not and ask why not? Imagination is relating the unrelated. Making new connections instead of old ones. How many new uses can you find for a paper clip? A brick? A wire coat hanger? A used tire? How many newer faster ways can you find to do old things?

Imagination is more important than knowledge.

—Albert Einstein

*People need your love the most
when they appear to deserve it the least.*

—John Harrigan

The greatest thing in this world is not so much where you stand as in what direction you are moving.

—Goethe

The greatest good we can do for others is not to share our riches but to reveal theirs.

And wouldn't that be the purpose of a manager as coach, too?!   I believe that one of the purposes of training programs and one of the jobs of a manager is to have people leave impressed with themselves - not intimidated by the instructor. Excited about what they now know that they didn't know before, what they can now do that they couldn't do before and with greater feeling and confidence in their abilities

The greatest good we can do for others is— not to share OUR riches— but to reveal THEIRS.

—Anonymous

If you can dream it, you can do it.

—Walt Disney

Great discoveries and achievements invariably involve the cooperation of many minds.

It takes people working together to get things done. Teamwork is the key. Uncovering talents and abilities, developing them, and focusing them toward a goal-- this ignites achievement far beyond any single person, no matter how brilliant or skilled.

Great discoveries and achievements invariably involve the cooperation of many minds.

—Anonymous

Eighty percent of success is showing up.

—Woody Allen

*No job on earth is insignificant
if it is accomplished
with pride and artistry.
"The french fry is my canvas,"
said McDonald's founder Ray Kroc.
What's your canvas?*

Trust your crazy ideas.

—Dan Zadra

There is no finish line.

Why not enjoy the process of life. Each day, each hour, each moment complete in itself. Focus on the here and now.

There is no finish line.

—Nike Corporation Motto

The human mind, once stretched by a new idea, never regains its original dimensions.

You cannot take away awareness. What an exciting concept! New ideas and activities create new awareness. Our mind stretches and grows - It does not shrink. Each new day is alive with potential.

The human mind, once stretched by a new idea, never regains its original dimensions.

—Oliver Wendell Holmes

Write it down. Written goals have a way of transforming wishes into wants; can'ts into cans; dreams into plans; and plans into reality. Don't just think it - ink it!

Paul Meyer said, "Writing crystalizes thought and thought produces action." The very act of writing starts to make tangible our dream. Once we've written down we can ask "Why aren't I there already?" This will crystalize the barriers. One at a time we can find our way over, under, around or through. Then set a target time for accomplishing each action and go for it! Because you've written it down you've got something you can measure - and each step you take reinforces and accelerates your achievements.

Write it down.
Written goals have a way
of transforming wishes into wants;
can'ts into cans;
dreams into plans;
and plans into reality.
Don't just think about it—ink it.

—Anonymous

Your past is not your potential. In any hour you can choose to liberate the future.

The past need not predict the future. The past is simply the past. At any hour we can choose a new course, create a new future. Humans alone, of all creatures have the power to choose.

Your past is not your potential. In any hour you can choose to liberate the future.

—Marilyn Ferguson

My interest is in the future...
because I am going to spend
the rest of my life there.

—Charles F. Kettering

*Why go into something
to test the waters?
Go into it
to make waves.*

—Anonymous

77

You can't turn back the clock, but you can wind it up again.

—Bonnie Prudden

Take Risks. You can't fall off the bottom.

The safest choice to take - don't. The safest advice - don't.
But with risk goes reward. We risk and learn. We modify,
adjust, adapt, and risk again. Four of the saddest words in
the world are "I wish I had..."

Take risks.
You can't fall off the bottom.

—Barbara Proctor

There are no shortcuts to any place worth going.

A man once came to me after a seminar and said "Goal setting sounds great, but I'm too old to achieve what I want". I asked what he wanted. He said, "To get my Ph.D." I asked how long it would take. He said, "Four years." "How old are you," I asked. "46" he said. "How old will you be in 4 years if you work toward it?" "50" he said. How old will you be if you don't? "50" he said. Sometimes the road ahead seems long, but each step takes us closer to the goal. A little progress each day ends up yielding big results.

There are no shortcuts to any place worth going.

—Beverly Sills

*If you love what you do,
you will never work
another day in your life.*

—Anonymous

*All things come
to those who
go after them.*

—Anonymous

Build it and they will come!

—'Field of Dreams'

When the best leader's work is done, the workers say, "We did it ourselves!"

—Anonymous

Plan ahead. It wasn't raining when Noah built the ark.

It's been said that 10 minutes of planning can save an hour
of execution. Take the time to ask yourself some what if's
now to save some time later.

Plan ahead. It wasn't raining when Noah built the ark.

—Anonymous

If you cannot do great things,
do small things in a great way.

—Napoleon Hill

When it is dark enough, you can see the stars.

—Emerson

What I cannot love, I overlook.

—Anais Nin

Working together works.

—Dr. Rob Gilbert

Alphabetical Phrase Reference

Vacuum Principle *45*

Order Form:

_____	Dreams Volume 1	$9.95
_____	Dreams Volume 2	$9.95
_____	Cheers	$5.95
_____	Smiles	$5.95

_____	Friends	$5.95
_____	Happiness	$5.95
_____	Thanks	$5.95

Name _____

Company_____

Street_____

City/State/Zip_____

Telephone (   )_____

Mail Orders to
Resources for Organizations, Inc.
7251 Flying Cloud Drive
Eden Prairie, MN 55344
Or Call   (612) 829-1954
Or Fax   (612) 829-0260

Order Information:
All orders must be prepaid.
Shipping and handling $0.75 per book.
MN & FL residents must add 6% sales tax.

Total amount due_____

Form of Payment:
_____   Check or money order
_____   Visa _____   MC
Card #_____
Exp Date._____
Signature_____

Dreams, V-1